How To Be Healed

Lawrence Thompson

Copyright © 2002 by Lawrence Thompson

How To Be Healed
by Lawrence Thompson

Printed in the United States of America

Library of Congress Control Number: 2002107761
ISBN 1-591601-35-5

All rights reserved. No part of this publication may be reproduced or transmitted in any form or by any means without written permission of the publisher.

Unless otherwise indicated, Bible quotations are taken from the King James Version. Published to the Public doman 1989 by Project Gutenburg.

Xulon Press
11350 Random Hills Road
Suite 800
Fairfax, VA 22030
(703) 279-6511
XulonPress.com

To order additional copies,
call 1-866-909-BOOK (2665).

Table of Contents

Chapter 1	Desiring God	7
Chapter 2	God's Desire for You	19
Chapter 3	You Must Trust the Word	27
Chapter 4	How Faith Works	35
Chapter 5	Hearing God's Voice	47
Chapter 6	The Gift of Faith	59
Chapter 7	The Confession of Faith	67
Chapter 8	The Origin of Sickness	77
Chapter 9	The Atonement	89
Chapter 10	Learning How to Receive	99
Chapter 11	How the Kingdom Works	105
Chapter 12	Let's Hear That Again	109
	Statement of Limitations	117
	Healing Log	119
	Author Contact	124

Chapter 1

Desiring God

How badly do you want it? You may think that there is nothing lacking in your desire for healing. Has your desire caused you to change your behavior? Have your patterns of prayer, bible study, and fellowship changed? Have you changed the way you make decisions about giving money? If your desire hasn't caused changes in your behavior, then either you don't need changes or your desire needs to be examined.

When my wife was hospitalized and near death I prayed, "Lord, I don't want anything to stand between my prayers for her and you." The answer I got back was, "Tithe." I had no job. The unemployment check in my hand was for only $339. My house payment was $670. My vehicle payments totaled $637. I had no idea how I would pay my bills. I wrote a check for $33.90 to give to our church. I still tithe, even though the emergency is past and she is a miracle survivor of a serious brain injury. There were other changes during this time. Each made in response to the voice of the Lord heard during prayer. Each confirmed by the scriptures.

I heard the story of a young man who went to a minister and said, "I want the same power in my ministry that you have in yours." The minister said, "Follow me." He got in his car and drove far into the country, stopping by a lake. He got out and walked toward the lake. At the edge of the water, he turned to the young man and said, "Follow me." He then walked out into the water. The young man followed. The minister grabbed the young man and held him under for a long time while he struggled to get free. He finally raised the young man up, sputtering water. "Are you trying to kill me?" asked the young man. The minister said, "When you desire God as much as you wanted that breath of air, you will have power to minister."

I don't know if the story is true or not. It sounds made-up. The point is, desire overrides all other motivations. If you want something badly enough, you will find it.

Please consider this example of desired healing from the Bible:

"And as they departed from Jericho, a great multitude followed him. And, behold, two blind men sitting by the way side, when they heard that Jesus passed by, cried out, saying, Have mercy on us, O Lord, thou son of David. And the multitude rebuked them, because they should hold their peace: but they cried the more, saying, Have mercy on us, O Lord, thou son of David. And Jesus stood still,

and called them, and said, What will ye that I shall do unto you?

They say unto him, Lord, that our eyes may be opened. So Jesus had compassion on them, and touched their eyes: and immediately their eyes received sight, and they followed him." (Matthew 20:29-34)

The two blind men shouted out to Jesus for healing. They didn't ask weakly. They shouted, creating something of a ruckus. They got healed. If healing depended on shouting, many today would stay sick. The same ones would be at the ball game screaming their lungs out. Maybe these two blind men discovered something we need. They risked being labeled total fools for the sake of the Master's touch. Get ready to shout.

In Mark's account, he tells of only one man, Bartimaeus (Mark 10:46). When he was told to be quiet, he shouted even louder. When he was told that Jesus was calling him, he threw off his cloak and came to Jesus. I don't know if you ever forgot a coat and left it somewhere where many people passed by. If you did, you probably didn't see that coat again. In Jesus' day, clothes were even more costly than they are today. Bartimaeus threw caution to the wind by abandoning his coat. We don't know what was on his mind. Comic insight might suggest that he knew he could spot anyone bothering his coat after he had his sight! Most likely he was so intent on getting what he needed from Jesus that he didn't want to slow down even to care for his possessions. Today we would call him foolish. He, however, regained his sight.

NOTE: TAKE TIME TO READ EACH SCRIPTURE REFERENCE!

"My son, attend to my words; incline thine ear unto my sayings. Let them not depart from thine eyes; keep them in the midst of thine heart. For they are life unto those that find them, and health to all their flesh." (Proverbs 4:20-22)

Proverbs tells us that God's words give life and health. There are no wiser words than those in the Bible. If you had simply read all the scriptures about healing again and again until you fully understood them, you would be writing and not reading. Whenever I get too busy and distracted with day-to-day living that I let sickness overtake me, I slow down and return to the Word. As I read the scriptures, faith enters into my heart and healing comes.

Many times people in this age hear Jesus calling but are held back by the things they hold dear. One will cling to a job, another to a house. One will hold tightly to a spouse, another to a child.

The first night of my wife's ordeal, I cried out, "Lord, save my girl!" He questioned, "Whose girl?" It then struck me that I was praying with a selfish desire, considering only what I wanted. I said, "Lord, your girl." As I released her to Him, I had a mental image of her in God's glory with His angels surrounding her. The next day, in the hospital chapel, I prayed, "Lord, I know she is in your hands, but I need to know if she will live or die." I heard Him saying, "She won't die, but will live and declare my works." I was drawn to the Bible on a stand at the front of the chapel. I approached the Bible, looked down, and flipped over a handful of pages. There before me were the words of a Psalm, speaking to my heart.

"The right hand of the Lord is exalted: the right hand of the Lord doeth valiantly. I shall not die, but live, and declare the works of the Lord." (Psalm 118:16-17)

I knew He was saying that my wife would live. Even at the risk of sounding crazy, I told the people waiting with me what He had spoken in my heart. When I was allowed to visit her in Intensive Care, I would bend over the bed, close to her face, and say, "You will not die, but live, and declare the works of the Lord." At this point, I was willing to have people think I was crazy if necessary to get help from the Lord. The fruit of such craziness is a woman who is able to function day to day. A woman who can drive anywhere she needs to and can do all that life requires of her. Not bad for someone who had a serious brain injury and several strokes.

Another woman, one with whom I worked, was unable to have children. The doctors had tried all they knew to do, even surgery. They gave her no hope. When she shared this situation with me, I told her I would pray for her to conceive. That night at home after my family was snug in bed, I got on my knees on the cement slab in the back room of our house and prayed. I told the Lord who I was praying for (as if He didn't know!). I told Him I wasn't going to get up from that spot until I heard from Him. I wasn't going to sleep and eat. I wasn't going to work. I was going to stay riveted to that spot in prayer for her until I heard Him speak. It was quite a long time later, after all feeling had left my knees and legs, that I heard the Spirit say, "It's done." At first I didn't understand, so He repeated, "It's done." Then I understood that the Lord was telling me that He heard my prayer and had granted what I had asked of Him. I remembered the scripture in John:

"And this is the confidence that we have in him, that, if we ask any thing according to his will, he heareth us: And if we know that he hear us, whatsoever we ask, we know that we have the petitions that we desired of him." (John 5:14-15)

I rejoiced because I knew I had prayed according to the Lord's will and knew He had heard me. I knew it was a done deal. I knew she would have a child. I would have gotten up and gone to bed except that my legs where so numb I couldn't move. I lay on the floor for a long time praising the Lord, suffering miserably as blood flowed back into my legs. Finally, I was able to get up and go to bed.

A short time later, the young woman saw me at work and almost exploded, "I'm pregnant!"

When we pray, we must have the kind of determined stance that says, "I'm not letting go until heaven and earth are moved." People of faith years ago referred to this as "praying through". Most people today are "through" before they "pray".

"And he spake a parable unto them to this end, that men ought always to pray, and not to faint; Saying, There was in a city a judge, which feared not God, neither regarded man: And there was a widow in that city; and she came unto him, saying, Avenge me of mine adversary. And he would not for a while: but afterward he said within himself, Though I fear not God, nor regard man; Yet because this widow troubleth me, I will avenge her, lest by her continual coming she weary me. And the Lord said, Hear what the unjust judge saith. And shall not God avenge his own elect, which cry day and night unto him, though he bear long with them? I tell you that he will avenge them speedily. Nevertheless when the Son of man cometh, shall he find faith on the earth?" (Luke 18:1-8)

It seems as if Jesus knew of our day, even two thousand year ago. We don't persevere. We don't persist. We often pray only after we have exhausted all other means of getting help. When you are lying in the hospital with your flesh rotting around you, it is not time to begin a life of prayer; it is time to make peace with God and man. If you haven't made the habit of calling out to God all along the way, you probably won't know where to find Him when you are slipping off a ledge. Does that mean that there is no hope for you unless you started praying years ago? Certainly not. It just may take a lot more effort. Once you get passed this ordeal, make the habit of prayer and trusting God so it will go easier for you next time. You will have fewer next times. You will also be able to share your abundance of health with others.

Praying with our heart's desire set on God may not yield what we are expecting, but if we pray without our heart's desire set on God, we are certain to fail in our search for help. Remember, GOD satisfies the desires of our hearts!

"Delight thyself also in the LORD: and he shall give thee the desires of thine heart. Commit thy way unto the LORD; trust also in him; and he shall bring it to pass." (Psalm 37:4-5)

The modern approach to God is to only embrace the portion of God with which you are comfortable. This is not God's way. Remember the first Passover, before the Israelites left Egypt? They were commanded to eat the whole lamb. Any portion left over was to be burned in the fire (Exodus 12:8-10). God doesn't let you decide when and where you will experience His presence in your life. When He says, "Here I am." He means, "Come NOW!" He also doesn't let you decide which parts of the Bible you will not believe. One person says, "I believe in Jesus, but I can't go for that healing stuff." Not only will that person miss out on healing, but that person will also miss out on many other blessing. You can't say, "I love Jesus" and practice racism. You can't say, "I obey God" and turn your back on hungry people. How many of you have pastors living at the poverty level because you did the math and figured out that a tithe of your income was as much as a house payment? There is an expression we once heard in Christian circles, "Jesus is Lord of all or not Lord at all." There was a lot of truth to that expression. If you are holding out on Jesus, stop. If you are grasping your life so tightly that God can't bless you, let go. You might have to learn to bless the people who cut you off in traffic. You might have to learn to manage your affairs on ninety percent of your income. Don't leave part of Jesus out of your life and He won't leave you out of part of His blessings.

If you miss out on God while He is calling, it may be a while before you hear Him call again. Once, while attending a business conference, I met a woman who told me about her dad's illness and her concerns for him. The Holy Spirit was continually prompting me to tell her about Jesus and to offer to pray for her dad. I was uncomfortable sharing my faith with business associates, so I failed to do so. For over a year, I was totally devoid of a sense of the Lord's presence. I knew He was there, but I felt nothing. If you are to experience the presence and glory of God, you must be eager to press in and seize hold of Him while He is available.

Sometimes, people intend to get serious with God, but they let the affairs of this life keep them too busy to make the effort.

Before I became a Christian, I was in Holland with an Army band to play for a memorial ceremony at a NATO cemetery. Afterwards, we went into town to eat. On the way back to the bus, a drunken man confronted me in the street. He repeatedly said, "Seek God while He may be found." Considering that I grew up in church without ever meeting Jesus and considering that I was heavily involved in occult religion and drugs, I was scared speechless. I couldn't get it out of my mind. Later I found that the Bible offers the same admonition (Isaiah 55:6). In the same way that stubborn Balaam had to hear of God's glory through his donkey (Numbers 22:28), I had to hear God's warning from the mouth of a drunk. From that time until I met Jesus, I walked about in fear that I wouldn't find Him before it was too late.

So now you are thinking, "I will change my ways to start having a quiet time with the Lord tomorrow." No! That is too late. The time of faith is today, never later. Don't wait until tomorrow. Get on your knees now and get started seeking God. You might as well start with repentance. I have never met anyone who couldn't find a single thing of which to repent. You also need to spend more time in praise and thanksgiving than you spend asking for stuff. This is the glorious Creator of all things! Not someone's interpretation of Santa. Until you have worshipped Him unashamed, you haven't gotten serious.

"O come, let us worship and bow down: let us kneel before the Lord our maker. For he is our God; and we are the people of his pasture, and the sheep of his hand. Today if ye will hear his voice . . . " (Psalm 95: 6-7)

Give yourself a quick test before you go on. Are you ready to do anything necessary to receive healing from God? Are you ready to obey Him? Did you take time to look up the scriptures referenced in this chapter and have you read and reread them? Take time to get very serious now so you can take advantage of the rest of this book. You won't be sorry.

Chapter 2

God's Desire for You

Most people are confused about God's desire for them. Some see God as an impersonal "Being", way off in some place called Heaven. Some see Him as smaller than their own brains. They think they have Him all figured out. Some believe in the gospel of abandonment. They think God gave us birth but won't have anything else to do with us until we die.

When it comes to healing, people have as many strange ideas about God's desire for us as there are people. Some think God never heals. Some say, "I didn't get healed, therefore God doesn't heal". Some say, "God heals some, but not all". The some-not-all crowd, when questioned about how to be in the some, indicate that it is a cosmic dice game. God rolls up His sleeves, blows on the dice, shakes them, says, "Baby needs a new pair of lungs." and lets them roll. Sometimes He gets a seven and baby lives. Some times it comes up snake eyes and baby dies.

The problem is that we tend to interpret the scriptures by our traditions and personal experiences. The intellectual name for this is Post-Modernism. One assumes that truth is only what "I" have experienced. There are many documents written by the theologians of our day embracing this position. I recently read a paper that said, "Tongues are not for this day because I don't speak in tongues and neither do a lot of seminary professors who know Greek and Hebrew." How arrogant it is to presume that only our experience is valid. What we should do instead is evaluate our traditions and personal experiences in the light of the scriptures.

If you speed through a school zone and are stopped by a patrolman, do you say, "Its ok because my car is capable of much greater speed than the posted speed limit"? If you do, he will write the ticket and then call for reinforcements, with white jackets. Most people would say such a response is crazy. Yet, that is the way most people approach the Bible.

The Bible tells us in Exodus 15:26, "…I am the Lord that healeth thee." From there until the last chapter, it never indicates a change in His heart desire toward us. The psalmist knew this and recited, "Bless the Lord, O my soul: and all that is within me, bless his holy name. Bless the Lord, O my soul, and forget not all his benefits: Who forgiveth all thine iniquities; who healeth all thy diseases;" (Psalm 103:1-3).

A little later we will explore the origin of sickness. For now, let me make the assumption that God is the cure. He never says, "I will heal some of your diseases". Anyone who ever asked Jesus for healing got it. When Paul was ship wrecked on Melita, the islanders brought their sick people to him and he healed all of them. If a rich man dies and leaves me all his fortune but I elect to only take $20, it doesn't mean that he didn't leave me all of it. It only means that I didn't receive all of it. The responsibility for receiving is always ours. God is not going to force His desire on us. He didn't create us to be robots, responding as He gives the command. He created us to be thinking, feeling creatures who respond to Him out of desire.

You might say, "But I have been taught that God puts sickness on us to teach us." While it is true that the Bible speaks of trials and difficulties, in the many times I have read and re-read the Bible, I have never found any reference to God putting disease on anyone except in cases of disobedience and wickedness. If you are convinced that this is your condition, give up the sin and submit your will to God so you can be healed. In fact, Proverbs 10:22 tells us that God's blessing enriches us and doesn't contain any sorrow. It appears that we can have it one of two ways, blessing (including healing), or cursing with its sorrows.

"But what about Job?"

The Bible doesn't say God made Job sick. Instead He stepped back. Satan came and afflicted Job.

"But God allowed it. Maybe God is allowing satan to afflict me."

Revelation 12:11 says we overcome satan by the "blood of the lamb" and by our testimony. If God were to step back from me in this moment, the application of the blood of the lamb, Jesus, to my heart through repentance of sin and humility before God would put the "hedge" of God about me. But, even if I become sick, for whatever reason, it doesn't change the truth that God doesn't desire for me to be that way. The lesson of Job is this: "Though he slay me, yet will I trust in him", Job 13:15. Job did not lose his confidence in God, even during his ordeal. We don't have to repeat the ordeal of Job because the lesson has been given. Never lose your confidence in God. Always trust Him, regardless of the circumstances.

Another way to understand God's desire toward us in regard to healing is to consider salvation of the lost. We know from 2 Peter 3:9 that God is not willing that any should perish. Do any perish? Most people would say yes. They would be in agreement with the Bible. Revelation 20:15 tells us that when the dead are judged, those whose names are not in the book of life will be cast into the lake of fire. If that isn't perishing, I don't know what is. What happens if we take the approach of judging God's desire based on experience? We must say that if some are lost, then God desired it. But the Bible says He doesn't desire it. So make up your mind. Will you believe tradition and experience or the Bible?

Years ago, I heard a preacher say, "God's not your problem." Another way of saying this is "God doesn't hold out on you." God desires to bless you with all good blessings. The Bible is full of assurances of this truth. We fail, corporately and individually, to share His blessings. If I tell my child,

"Don't eat the whole box of chocolate" and he sneaks it into his room and eats it all, it doesn't mean that I desired for him to have a tummy ache. Sometimes God's children don't follow His instructions. Then they get tummy aches. Then they blame God. Sounds pretty stupid doesn't it. Anybody got a mirror.

The 28th chapter of Deuteronomy tells us of the blessing we will get if we obey God. The passage then goes on to tell us what will happen to us if we don't obey God. The list is extensive. Even so, it goes even farther by saying every disease and plague not listed will be ours as well. God takes obedience seriously. Many people desire healing, but are unwilling to forgive others. Other people are stingy. Some are backbiters. Some point their fingers in scorn. They have earned their sickness through disobedience. Why should God spite Himself and remove the curse He promised for their disobedience. If they would repent, turning away from their sin, they could be healed.

How else do I know God wants me healed? James 5:14-15 says:

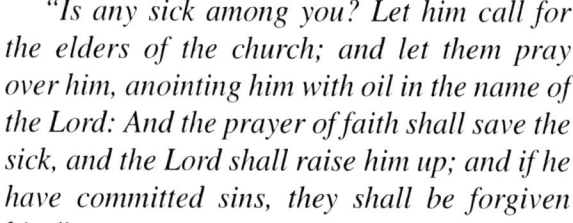

"Is any sick among you? Let him call for the elders of the church; and let them pray over him, anointing him with oil in the name of the Lord: And the prayer of faith shall save the sick, and the Lord shall raise him up; and if he have committed sins, they shall be forgiven him."

If God didn't want you well, He wouldn't tell you what to do when you are sick. You may say, "My church doesn't have elders." You may not have people bearing the official title, but there are probably people who are mature and walk upright before the Lord. If they also believe God desires to heal you, they are your elders. This scripture says the prayer of faith will save the sick. I have seen people designated as elders by title because they gave a lot of money to the church or because they agreed with everything the pastor said. These are not your elders.

Elders are spiritual. They have a sure knowledge of God's desire toward you. Find elders who believe God desires to heal and have them pray for you. When Peter went to pray for Dorcas, he put the people out of the room before he called her back to life (Acts 9:40). In this he followed Jesus' example as shown in Matthew 9:25. When Jesus told the people the girl was not dead, they laughed at Him. Jesus put them out of the room and raised her up. You would do well to put people out of the room who don't believe. If they think you are silly or weak minded for seeking healing from God, send them away before you pray. If all they want to pray is for you to have strength to endure, send them away and pray for God's gift to make you whole. There sometimes seem to be more scoffers than believers when you need help and they don't.

Dwight L. Moody preached a sermon about atheists where he noted that when they are on their deathbeds or their loved ones are dying, they don't send for other atheists to give them comfort. They seek out believers. Follow their example, for in their fear, they are following the example Peter learned from Jesus.

It is not enough to mentally acknowledge that God is capable of healing. It is not enough to want healing. All but the seriously disturbed want healing. Most don't get it. You must also be willing to believe that God wants you well. When Jesus referred to God as "Abba, Father" (Mark 14:36), He indicated that God is a familiar, caring person. He is our "Daddy". Jesus said that God is an even better Father than we are. We don't give our children stones when they ask for bread (Matthew 7:9), why should God?

The reason our society considers God to be a stranger or an enemy is because we have made ourselves to be His enemy. It is true that you can't have everything your way and get God's best. Until you are tired of getting what you want, you won't do what is necessary to get God's blessing. You won't obey Him. "How do I obey Him?" you ask. Start at the beginning and "Love one another" (John 13:34). Then read the New Testament. Each time you find a commandment from the Lord, do it. If we all did this, we wouldn't be crying about healing.

The following chapters of this book will walk you through the process of receiving healing from God. If you have become convinced that God wants you healed and have committed to do what ever it takes to receive His healing, there is no reason why you cannot receive it.

Chapter 3

You Must Trust the Word

When I hear two theologians arguing about the integrity of the scriptures, I mentally picture two men, standing in the rain, arguing about the advantages of hats versus umbrellas and having neither at their disposal. Every theologian has an opinion about the integrity of the scriptures, but few avail themselves of the treasures therein.

There seem to be three basic camps. Those who believe the Bible is 100% literally true with no margin for error or human discrepancy, those who believe the Bible to be inspired of God, written by man, and a revelation of truth, and those who believe that the Bible is a myth.

If you believe that the Bible is a myth, you probably should quit now. The odds of your getting healed are negligible. Even Jesus was hampered in His miracle working ability in His home town because of their unbelief.

How To Be Healed

"...And he did not many mighty works there because of their unbelief." (Matthew 13:58)

Later I will explore the fact that faith comes as a gift as the Word of God enters into our spirits. The only sources we have for hearing the Word are the Bible and by hearing voices. If you choose to hear voices, you risk being deceived unless you have something to verify their message, namely, the Bible. If you are not willing to concede that the Bible is used by God to speak to us, then you will severely hamper your efforts to have faith and thereby to be healed.

Someone once told me, "We had faith, and grandmother died anyway." While I don't presume to guarantee that I could have kept your grandmother alive, I question the existence of that faith and wonder about the presence of unbelief. Often people have desire or presumption. They want a miracle or they think they can have one because "they are as good as anyone else." Do I believe every failure to be healed is because of a lack of faith? No. I only insist that the problem is never with God's desire or ability to heal.

When we get a miracle it is because God says it, we believe it, and we act accordingly.

Consider the role of the Word in healing as found in the scriptures:

"He sent his word, and healed them, and delivered them from their destructions. " (Psalms 107:20)

❦

"My son, attend to my words; incline thine ear unto my sayings. Let them not depart from thine eyes; keep them in the midst of thine heart. For they are life unto those that find them, and health to all their flesh." (Proverbs 4:20-22)

It isn't too strange that the Bible says God's words are life to our flesh. God started the whole thing with a word. John's gospel tells us that the Word existed in the beginning and created all things. Nothing was created except by the Word.

❦

"In the beginning was the Word, and the Word was with God, and the Word was God. The same was in the beginning with God. All things were made by him; and without him was not any thing made that was made. " (John 1:1-3)

When we read as far as Revelation, we see that Jesus is Himself called the "Word of God".

❦

"And I saw heaven opened, and behold a white horse; and he that sat upon him was called Faithful and True, and in righteousness he doth judge and make war. His eyes were as a flame of fire, and on his head were many crowns; and he had a name written, that no

man knew, but he himself. And he was clothed with a vesture dipped in blood: and his name is called The Word of God. And the armies which were in heaven followed him upon white horses, clothed in fine linen, white and clean. And out of his mouth goeth a sharp sword, that with it he should smite the nations: and he shall rule them with a rod of iron: and he treadeth the winepress of the fierceness and wrath of Almighty God. And he hath on his vesture and on his thigh a name written, KING OF KINGS, AND LORD OF LORDS." (Revelation 19:11-16)

The Bible is a revelation of Jesus from start to finish. The words God spoke to reveal His son have life. They are effective in doing the task He sent them to do.

"So shall my word be that goeth forth out of my mouth: it shall not return unto me void, but it shall accomplish that which I please, and it shall prosper in the thing whereto I sent it." (Isaiah 55:11)

The Old Testament was given for instruction. It contains the Law of God. The Law does not make us better, it just tells us how bad we are. The Israelites turned back and forth from worshipping God to worshipping objects made by man. In their error, God allowed them to be carried off into slavery. In their captivity, they remembered God and called out to Him again. God delivered them from slavery and restored possession of their own land. This process was repeated over and over again until Israel finally learned, "Hear, O Israel: The LORD our God is one LORD." (Deuteronomy 6:4). The Old Testament is a record of these things.

When Jesus came, He lived by the teachings of the Old Testament. Jesus learned the Law of God and obeyed it. He was the only man who ever succeeded in keeping the Law. The reason He succeeded is that He understood that God is God of the heart. Sin originates in the heart. So does righteousness. Jesus lived a life free from sin because He knew God's heart and was thereby able to keep God's Law. When the time was right, He became the sacrifice for our sin. Because He didn't deserve to die, His sacrifice wasn't used up by His own sin. It remains today sufficient for mine as well.

These are the things of the Bible. That is why the enemies of God and God's people don't want you to know the Word of God and to believe in it's integrity. You see, they are afraid that you will have God's word in your heart and stop sinning.

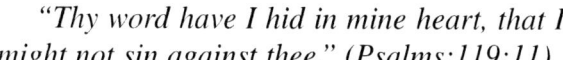

"Thy word have I hid in mine heart, that I might not sin against thee." (Psalms:119:11)

Then nothing can stop you from being blessed by God. The world wants the power to decide what to do more than they want blessing. They pollute the

Word of God because it requires walking a narrow line of obedience to God. Out of that obedience comes blessing, including healing.

"Behold, the LORD's hand is not shortened, that it cannot save; neither his ear heavy, that it cannot hear: But your iniquities have separated between you and your God, and your sins have hid his face from you, that he will not hear". (Isaiah 59:1-2)

So what of the Bible? Can you accept it as authority? Answer this; do you have any other authority that you know can heal you?

Doctors don't heal. They cut away disease (surgery), kill diseased cells with chemical poisons (ex. Chemotherapy), dispense substances that mimic the body's own defenses (antibiotics), and apply various other treatments and therapies in hopes that the body will gain an edge over disease and the marvelous bio-machine you live in will kick start it's immune system and recover. I don't mean this to belittle doctors. I thank the men and women of science who sacrifice their time continually studying medicine and sacrifice their own health working long tiring hours making every effort to bring you to health. I just think that a proper perspective on medicine is good medicine. There is so very little we yet know about the body and how to heal it. We still struggle to understand many common ailments.

You Must Trust the Word

There is a certain freedom in admitting our limitations. If my comments have hurt any medical professional, I apologize, but I am more intent on getting you to move the short distance toward faith that will bring true healing.

Get used to me saying that the Word works. Apart from God's promise, there is very little hope for us.

Jesus often cited faith as the reason for healing.

"Then touched he their eyes, saying, According to your faith be it unto you. And their eyes were opened; and Jesus straitly charged them, saying, ..." (Matthew 9:30)

Paul let us know where faith comes from.

"So then faith cometh by hearing, and hearing by the word of God." (Romans 10:17)

Make a heart commitment to read the Bible and let it speak to you. Remember that Jesus is the Word. He is a living Word. When you hear the living Word, faith will come. Take a chance and trust the Word. What have you got to lose. Oh yes, your disease.

Chapter 4

How Faith Works

The Bible says you can't please God without faith (Hebrews 11:6). Everything we receive from God comes by faith. You might try to live a good life, motivating yourself with a knowledge of God, but you will only experience His blessing first hand if you exercise faith. Faith isn't hard to understand. Faith isn't hard to get. You may have to change what you think about faith in order to get faith. Change your mind. It is worth it. The reward of faith is always delivered by God's own hand. You can't have faith and not see results.

Many people start teaching faith by quoting the eleventh chapter of Hebrews.

"Now faith is the substance of things hoped for, the evidence of things not seen." (Hebrews 11:1).

It may be just as important to quote Webster's New World Dictionary of the American Language.

"FAITH...1 unquestioning belief that does not require proof or evidence."

Notice that the Bible does not say that faith is being sure of what we have. Once you see, taste, hear, feel, or smell it, no more faith is required, unless some doubt makes you distrust your senses. Many times people receive something from God and then doubt their senses, only to loose the blessing they had received. Doubt is negative faith. Doubt, like fear, is faith that something bad or undesirable will happen. Faith is a certain knowledge that does not require proof. When faith enters your heart (your spirit) and convinces your mind, no further evidence is required. That is why the Bible says; faith is the evidence or certainty of what we do not see.

How can you have faith without seeing? Something beyond our normal experience must happen for us to believe what we cannot see. You might have a friend promise to pick you up after work and take you home. In the back of your mind you have a "Plan B". If the friend doesn't show, you will catch a ride with someone else, call a taxi, or just plain walk. You never truly rely on absolute faith when dealing with the things normal to the earth. When dealing with the things normal only to God, there is no room for a "Plan B", only a "Plan J", Jesus, who could not fail, did not fail, and will not fail me now.

If you truly know what God desires, you can be assured that He will provide. The first step is to know what God desires.

"And this is the confidence that we have in him, that, if we ask any thing according to his will, he heareth us: And if we know that he hear us, whatsoever we ask, we know that we have the petitions that we desired of him." (1 John 5:14-15).

If we ask according to His will, we have what we ask. James wrote,

"Ye ask, and receive not, because ye ask amiss, that ye may consume it upon your lusts." (James 4:3).

You must know what God wants you to have and how He wants you to use it. Then you must ask with the true desire to use it as He desires. If these conditions are met, you will receive. Many people quote:

"So then faith cometh by hearing, and hearing by the word of God." (Romans 10:17)

Faith does come after hearing occurs. This is not just hearing with your ear. The word must enter your spirit. You can play tapes of the Bible over and over and not receive faith. You must look up to God with the true desire to use what He gives as He desires. Then the miracle happens, God puts faith in your spirit.

Faith is a gift from God. Ephesians 2:8-9 tells us,

"For by grace are ye saved through faith; and that not of yourselves: it is the gift of God: Not of works, lest any man should boast."

Every instance of faith comes as a gift from God. It comes after you entertain the words of God in your mind and desire His will in your heart. Then, as you expectantly wait for God, He will put the gift of faith in your heart. If man could generate faith by his own actions, then the grace of God would not be required for salvation. The Bible clearly tells us that salvation is a gift from God. The Bible just as clearly tells us that salvation requires belief, or faith. God requires that we consider His truth or words. He then requires that we desire His will for us. As we wait expectantly, without wavering, He will answer with the gift of faith in our hearts (spirits) that will enable us to receive what we need from Him. When this faith comes into our spirits, we believe we have already received from Him. We then confess our faith.

For salvation, the Bible instructs,

"But what saith it? The word is nigh thee, even in thy mouth, and in thy heart: that is, the word of faith, which we preach; That if thou shalt confess with thy mouth the Lord Jesus, and shalt believe in thine heart that God hath raised him from the dead, thou shalt be saved.

For with the heart man believeth unto righteousness; and with the mouth confession is made unto salvation." (Romans 10:8-10).

Notice that the Bible does not say that it is with your mind that you believe. Your mind may know, but it will never believe. Most people fail at faith because they do not recognize that they have a spirit capable of faith. When faith comes, your mind will be convinced, even without evidence. This will take place through your spirit or heart. The Bible calls the spirit the heart. Sometimes, the certainty of faith will seem to be in your chest or stomach. This is your spirit receiving the faith that God gives.

Jesus said:

"He that believeth on me, as the scripture hath said, out of his belly shall flow rivers of living water." (John 7:38).

The King James translation of the Bible says that these streams will flow "out of his belly". The Revised Standard Version of the Bible says that these rivers will flow "out of his heart". The word translated means literally, belly, or inner most place. This is not the mind. The rivers of life God gives will never flow out of your mind. Faith from God will never flow into your mind. The mind is simply a storehouse of knowledge. The mind must be renewed to meditate on God's words. Then, as we turn our hearts to God, faith comes.

An important element of faith is perseverance. The Canaanite woman came to Jesus asking for healing for her daughter. Jesus didn't answer. She pressed in. Jesus responded to her determination and released the power she sought to get her daughter healed.

Jesus said:

" ..., O woman, great is thy faith: be it unto thee even as thou wilt...." (Matthew 15:28).

When you stand praying, don't stop until you get the gift of faith in your heart from God. Some people have called this praying until you receive the assurance or praying through. This is an important step that many people try to leave out. They try to jump to the next step and attempt to manufacture faith. It won't work.

Once the assurance is given and faith from God is poured into your spirit, you must confess the provision of God. We confess our salvation even though it has only begun and has not been completed yet. Our salvation will not be completed until Jesus returns and we are transformed into His image. We still confess our salvation. Are we lying? No! We have faith as our evidence. When we pray to God for anything that is in agreement with His will as revealed in the scriptures, we receive faith in our hearts from Him. Then we must take the next step which is the confession of faith in the thing which God has promised.

This is summed up in Mark 11:22-24,

"And Jesus answering saith unto them, Have faith in God. For verily I say unto you, That whosoever shall say unto this mountain, Be thou removed, and be thou cast into the sea; and shall not doubt in his heart, but shall believe that those things which he saith shall come to pass; he shall have whatsoever he saith. Therefore I say unto you, What things soever ye desire, when ye pray, believe that ye receive them, and ye shall have them."

You must speak to that mountain and not doubt in your heart. You must tell it to go. You must believe that you have received it and then it will be yours. Believing always precedes receiving. So lets get started; believe, confess, and receive!

To further explore faith, we can turn to any of the Biblical records of faith. One of my favorites is the story of Naaman, the leper, as recorded in 2 Kings 5:1-14. Naaman received his first word about possible healing through a young slave girl. It is interesting that a high commander in a conquering army would believe a slave girl's testimony. It is also interesting that she would bother to care about her captor. God often provides instruction for us from unlikely sources. You might be given a word from the Lord through a person that you know doesn't have your depth of knowledge or experience.

A total stranger, a drunken one at that, stopped me on a street in a small Dutch town and told me, "You'd better seek God while you can." I wasn't a

Christian at the time, but I was soon after. Now, more than thirty years later, I still remember his words and go seeking the Lord before I need Him. Somehow, that word touched me and extends even into my future, advising me to seek God while things are going well instead of following the normal religious model of calling on God when great need arises and only after exhausting all possible sources of help by the hand of man.

Naaman did receive the word and went to Israel. Like so many of us needing the touch of God, he went to man for help. He went to the king of Israel. There was no help for him there. Finally, the man of God sent word that the king was to send Naaman to him. He said, ".. he shall know that there is a prophet in Israel." (2 Kings 5:8). God works signs and wonders by faith to bear witness to His salvation (Hebrews 2:4). He sends the needy to His man or woman on every occasion so that He can exhibit His abilities. He desires that no one should perish because of a lack of knowledge of God.

When Naaman finally found himself at Elisha's house, Elisha sent a messenger to tell him what to do to be healed. He instructed Naaman to wash in the river Jordan. He didn't even get to see the prophet face to face. He was sent to dip in a muddy river. It wasn't the grandeur expected by a military commander. Naaman became mad. Often people don't receive from God because He requires something of them that insults their petty pride or wounds their human dignity. Once again Naaman heard from a servant. His own servants told him, "Wash and be cleansed." Naaman went to the river Jordan, dipped himself seven times, just as Elisha instructed, and was completely cleansed of leprosy. Only when he humbled himself and did what God required did he receive from God.

You can't sit still and receive from God. You must reach up to Him. Once the faith of God is deposited in your heart, you can't sit still. You must rise up and bear witness to what God has already done in you based on the evidence of your faith. Many times God's power to complete the work is released as some active step is taken. The blind man, Bartemaeus, we read about in Mark 10:46-52 was calling out, "Son of David, have mercy on me." People told him to be quiet, but he persevered and called out all the more. Finally he threw off his cloak and went toward Jesus. Bartemaeus was already seeing with his spirit. He moved toward Jesus, expecting to be healed. Jesus did heal him. Jesus then told him, "...your faith has healed you." What are you willing to let go of to move toward Jesus today? Which of your earthly treasures are you willing to drop in the crowd as you move forward, seeing only Jesus? Are you willing to let the crowd voice their disapproval as you press in to find Jesus? Just do it! They don't have to live with your pain or discouragement.

So we see that faith follows these steps. Find out what God wants for you. Hear the word. Meditate on that word until it becomes believable to you. Then ask God for what you desire, with your heart's desire aligned to agree with God's desire for you. Make your request in prayer until you have the certainty that He has granted the petition you make of Him. Smith Wigglesworth said that a man praying five times prayed four times in unbelief. This may be true. The important point is to continue praying until you know that you have been heard and God has answered. Begin to give thanks to God for His answer. Begin to witness His provision before men.

Continue in this mode without wavering and I guarantee that what you have sought will be yours.

Jesus backs up this guarantee,

" Ye have not chosen me, but I have chosen you, and ordained you, that ye should go and bring forth fruit, and that your fruit should remain: that whatsoever ye shall ask of the Father in my name, he may give it you. These things I command you, that ye love one another." (John 15:16-17).

How can you fail when you agree with God? Your confession is a step of faith. Make any other step of faith you believe is necessary. Seek the leading of the Holy Spirit. Paul said no man instructed him, meaning that the Holy Spirit taught him. Proverbs says there is wisdom in many counselors. Balance what other people tell you with what the Spirit of Jesus is saying in your heart.

Never forget that the time of faith is Today. You can't receive today what you believed in yesterday. You can't receive today what you plan to believe tomorrow. You can only receive today what you believe today. Years ago, my wife and I visited a small church of one of the older dominations that believes in the baptism in the Holy Spirit. The people were so excited to have guests that they put on quite a show for us. One woman shook as if in convulsions and the pastor ran around the church. After the meeting, the condition of the church was summed up by one woman who said, "My grandmother used to have the Spirit." They still did the visible things that where observed when the Holy Spirit visited years before in power, only now they were just mimicking what they had seen then.

The time of faith is Today. If you will read the fourth chapter of Hebrews, you will see that God set a day for His people to enter His rest. He called that day today.

People who enter into faith do indeed enter the Lord's rest. The battles are fought for the people of faith. They are clothed like the flowers of the field. They are fed like the birds of the air. They are at rest because the Spirit of the One who loved them and gave Himself for them is constantly at work satisfying the needs of their lives as they remain in the rest of the Lord. This is not to say that we stop doing anything. It is just to say that we stop struggling in the things we do, carefully picking our tasks to conform to all we know our Lord desires.

One last point about faith will serve you well. The enemy of my faith has tested everything I have received from God by trying to steal away my blessing. Sometimes I lost my blessing. Other times, I hung on in desperation. Almost every new Christian goes through a phase where they are not sure they have received God's salvation. Almost every person healed or otherwise touched by God later has doubts. There is a truth that will help you survive the testing of the evil one and keep the blessing you have received. Faith is a living thing.

James told us:

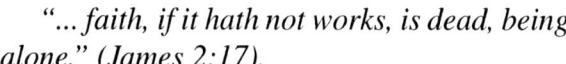

"... faith, if it hath not works, is dead, being alone." (James 2:17).

James was specifically referring to the necessity of benevolent works for your faith to remain alive. The many things you do because of the living spirit in you keep your faith alive. The one thing that helps me most with my faith, after being sure I pour out the love of Jesus in word and deed to other people, is to pray and sing in the Spirit. There is something about the use of tongues and the presence of the Holy Spirit that drives away the doubts and confusion. The enemy can't pull down a heart filled to bursting with the Spirit of Jesus and lips constantly uttering His praises. It is very difficult, if not impossible, to keep faith alive without the praises of God. Praying and singing in the Spirit helps keep that faith alive.

Remember! Without faith it is impossible to please God.

Chapter 5

Hearing God's Voice

The scripture tells us that we need to hear the God's word to be healed.

"My son, attend to my words; incline thine ear unto my sayings. Let them not depart from thine eyes; keep them in the midst of thine heart. For they are life unto those that find them, and health to all their flesh." (Proverbs 4: 20-22)

Even more important is for us to hear that the word relates directly to us. This I refer to as hearing God's voice. If you read a sweepstake entry form that says you can win a million dollars, you hear the words of the sponsors. If they call you and tell you that your entry won, you hear their voice. Many people memorize scripture and that is good. It is of greater importance, however, to hear the voice of God through the person of His Spirit telling you that a particular scripture is at that moment applied to you.

The scriptures have many references to the voice of God. We are told by 1 John 5:14 that if we pray according to God's will, we will have what we ask. This is the very model that Jesus followed. Jesus told his disciples, "... I do nothing of myself; but as my Father hath taught me." (John 8:28). This is our example through Jesus, our Lord. Hear the Father and do what He tells us to do. The scriptures tell us that the voice of the Father, otherwise known as the Word of God, is life and health to us. Many people want to hear God, and many others think they hear God. It is time, according to God's plan, for the church of Jesus to hear more clearly as each day passes. As we approach the time of Jesus' return we should become more and more capable of serving Him. The scriptures tell us "The counsel of the LORD standeth for ever,..." Psalms 33:11. How will we know His plan if we do not listen to His voice?

Modern Christians have adopted the humanist position that our talents and thoughts are of great worth. If you watch a Christian television program, you are likely to see celebrities who "came to the Lord". We have our own music "stars" who make millions of dollars with "Christian" music. I am not against Christian music. On the contrary, I enjoy it very much. I just don't like Christian people substituting entertainment for worship.

Our fascination with human value goes even deeper. We are delighted when a beauty pageant winner confesses on network television that she made it this far with the "help of the Lord". Then, a famous football player tells us how God helped him overcome drug addiction and become the best tackle in the NFL. Or maybe it's just a famous doctor telling us how the faith of his mother helped him rise from poverty to become the leading surgeon in the nation. Giving nominal lip service to the Lord has become a popular thing to do. Almost every famous entertainer will say a "God bless you" before returning to the motel for a night of debauchery.

Many drunken or high musicians stagger to the stage and sing "Amazing Grace" for the crowd. Wake up Christians! Amazing Grace with Jack Daniel's dripping from your mouth? I don't think so. God gives blessing to the humble. He lifts up the lowly and presses down the mighty. Why do we engage in fleshy hero worship? Is it not because we insist on being responsible for our own thoughts? Do we not refuse to yield our minds to the Holy Spirit?

The Holy Spirit must become the primary influence of our thoughts. Jesus told his disciples the source of Godly words.

"For it is not ye that speak, but the Spirit of your Father which speaketh in you." (Matthew 10:20)

This was not a new experience. Even before Jesus was born, Godly men and women spoke by the Holy Spirit.

"And it came to pass, that, when Elisabeth heard the salutation of Mary, the babe leaped in her womb; and Elisabeth was filled with the Holy Ghost: And she spake out with a loud voice, and said, Blessed art thou among women, and blessed is the fruit of thy womb." (Luke 1:41-42)

"Until the day in which he was taken up, after that he through the Holy Ghost had given commandments unto the apostles whom he had chosen:" (Acts 1:2)

Jesus gave His disciples instruction by the Holy Spirit. As He is our example, we should seek to speak words provided by God through His Holy Spirit. This is rarely good enough for us because we want the importance of providing the thoughts and words ourselves. We rarely give a Nobel peace prize to the person who listened to another's discovery and simply repeats it for us.

Human kind rewards the original, or at least the one who passes himself off as the original. God rewards the plagiarist, except He removes the plagiarism by claiming us as His own and giving us ownership of His words.

The apostles whose experiences are recorded in Acts spoke as the Holy Spirit gave them the words to say. These were men without degrees who were limited in their ability to use words and thoughts. God chose fisherman and such so we could see that He provides all we lack to do His pleasure.

"Then Peter, filled with the Holy Ghost, said unto them,..." (Acts 4:8)

The scriptures tell us the end result of retaining control of our thoughts versus the rewards of yielding to His Holy Spirit.

"For to be carnally minded is death; but to be spiritually minded is life and peace. Because the carnal mind is enmity against God: for it is not subject to the law of God, neither indeed can be." (Romans 8:6-7)

"But ye are not in the flesh, but in the Spirit, if so be that the Spirit of God dwell in you." (Romans 8:9)

"For as many as are led by the Spirit of God, they are the sons of God." (Romans 8:14)

The Spirit resides in the Heart of Man

To begin experiencing the voice of God by His Holy Spirit, it is necessary to understand where the Spirit resides. Man is a triune creation. He has spirit, soul, and body, as testified by the scriptures.

"For the word of God is quick, and powerful, and sharper than any two edged sword, piercing even to the dividing asunder of soul and spirit, and of the joints and marrow, and is a discerner of the thoughts and intents of the heart." (Hebrews 4:12)

Man's body is the physical organ in which he lives. It has no thoughts apart from the mind. It has no desires apart from the mind. It only exists and must be cared for with wisdom if it is to endure. Man's mind is the seat of his soul. It is from the mind that our thoughts and feelings spring forth. Man tends to think very highly of his own mind, thinking that no greater intellect exists. You may have heard of some incredible plan from a public figure and responded with, "Who does he think he is." The answer is simple; he thinks he is a great intellect. We all do. The mind is a powerful, creative tool. If it is used wisely, it is a great servant. If it is allowed to run the show, it becomes a destroyer. The destruction may take awhile, but it will come. Why, then, do men rely so heavily on their minds? Because their spirits are dead. Any spirit separated from God is dead. When our spirits are joined with the Spirit of God (1 Corinthians 6:17), we become spiritually alive. It is out of our spirits that life begins to flow.

"He that believeth on me, as the scripture hath said, out of his belly shall flow rivers of living water." (John 7:38)

The Spirit of God is deposited in our spirits making us alive. The Bible refers to the spirit as the heart many times. We know this because of the agreement of 1 Corinthians 6:17 and 2 Corinthians 1:21-22. The Spirit of God joins to our spirits. We are thereby sealed with the Spirit as a guarantee of God's promised salvation. This place of deposit is the heart of man, not his mind.

"Now he which stablisheth us with you in Christ, and hath anointed us, is God; Who hath also sealed us, and given the earnest of the Spirit in our hearts. (2 Corinthians 1:21-22)

"But he that is joined unto the Lord is one spirit." (1 Corinthians 6:17)

It is here, in our hearts or inner beings, that the Holy Spirit begins to work the edification of God. He builds us up, making us strong. Not through intellect, but through His presence in our spirits.

"That he would grant you, according to the riches of his glory, to be strengthened with

might by his Spirit in the inner man;" (Ephesians 3:16)

The Spirit is contrary to the sinful nature.

The only way to do God's good pleasure is to follow the dictates of His Spirit, joined with our spirits, directing our minds. Our minds provide our human desires, which run contrary to God's desires.

"See then that ye walk circumspectly, not as fools, but as wise, Redeeming the time, because the days are evil. Wherefore be ye not unwise, but understanding what the will of the Lord is. And be not drunk with wine, wherein is excess; but be filled with the Spirit;" (Ephesians 5:15-18).

"So I say, live by the Spirit, and you will not gratify the desires of the sinful nature. For the sinful nature desires what is contrary to the Spirit, and the Spirit what is contrary to the sinful nature. They are in conflict with each other, so that you do not do what you want. But if you are led by the Spirit, you are not under law. The acts of the sinful nature are obvious: sexual immorality, impurity and debauchery; idolatry and witchcraft; hatred, discord, jealousy, fits of rage, selfish ambition, dissensions, factions and envy; drunkenness, orgies, and the like. I warn you, as I did

before, that those who live like this will not inherit the kingdom of God. But the fruit of the Spirit is love, joy, peace, patience, kindness, goodness, faithfulness, gentleness and self-control. Against such things there is no law. Those who belong to Christ Jesus have crucified the sinful nature with its passions and desires. Since we live by the Spirit, let us keep in step with the Spirit." (Galatians 5:16-22)

So where is the voice of God?

"The LORD said, "Go out and stand on the mountain in the presence of the LORD, for the LORD is about to pass by." Then a great and powerful wind tore the mountains apart and shattered the rocks before the LORD, but the LORD was not in the wind. After the wind there was an earthquake, but the LORD was not in the earthquake. After the earthquake came a fire, but the LORD was not in the fire. And after the fire came a gentle whisper." (1 Kings 19:11-12)

God's voice is a gentle whisper. It comes up from our inner beings. It does not originate in our minds but passes through our spirits to our minds. When we hear God in our minds, but we only have a one-in-four chance of being correct. Our minds hear the words of God, hear our own thoughts, hear the voices of other people, and receive the whispers of our spiritual enemies. We should learn to hear the voice that comes up from our "bellies", or inner beings. This requires a quiet mind, a heart turned toward God with humility, and a burning desire to be with the Lord.

Finally, it takes faith to hear God. Jesus said we would know His voice and follow Him. We must trust Him and take Him at His word. Our lack of understanding is no excuse to use our minds to keep control of our "religious" experience. We must relinquish control to the Spirit of Jesus residing in us if we are to follow Jesus.

"My sheep listen to my voice; I know them, and they follow me. I give them eternal life, and they shall never perish; no one can snatch them out of my hand." (John 10:27-28)

Giving control of our minds to the Holy Spirit does not "unhook" our minds, but rather makes them the receivers and processors of the information communicated to us by the Spirit of God. The mind is the repository of this information. It organizes the information. In the mind, we lay out the plans God gives us. This makes the mind a tool, not the master of our destiny with God.

One of the biggest struggles in the church of today is the struggle to retain control with our minds. Because of our great ignorance of spiritual things, we allow our fear of the unknown to drive us to seize control and grasp it tightly. This is why so many churches are cursed with power struggles. If we let the Spirit be in control, what is there to fight for? If we let Him control our minds as the scripture directs, we gain the wisdom of God. If God speaks to us, will He speak stupidity? No! He will speak wisdom. Decide to hear the whispered voice of God in your spirit. You will have to get alone and spend time in prayer and worship, then quiet time listening. You, the sheep, will know His voice, just like He promised.

Chapter 6

The Gift of Faith

There has been much talk about spiritual gifts. This talk has caused some confusion regarding the gifts of the Spirit. If you believe you have an extraordinary ability to do something because the Lord has enabled you, that doesn't mean that it is a gift of the Spirit. I know people who have exceptional musical or theatrical ability that seems to be enhanced by the Lord. These are not the gifts of the Spirit. The may well be gifts, but these are gifts that typically involved a lot of human preparation. While it is true that our ability to allow the gifts of the Spirit to manifest well may require experience, the gift itself is complete without our human ability.

There are nine gifts of the Spirit listed in the Bible.

"But the manifestation of the Spirit is given to every man to profit withal. For to one is given by the Spirit the word of wisdom; to another the word of knowledge by the same Spirit; To another faith by the same Spirit; to

> *healing by the same Spirit;*
> *...ing of miracles; to another*
> *...ther discerning of spirits; to*
> *...nds of tongues; to another the*
> *...of tongues:"* (1 Corinthians

Teachers often divide the gifts into three groups by type of manifestation:

1. The revelation gifts
   a. word of wisdom (revelation of what to do)
   b. word of knowledge (revelation of previously unknown facts)
   c. discerning (or distinguishing) of spirits (identifying the culprit)

2. The gifts of utterance or speaking
   a. Prophecy (inspired utterance to strengthen, build up, and encourage)
   b. Tongues (or unlearned languages, whether human origin or not).
   c. Interpretation of tongues (a repeat of what was said in tongues, but in a language that has been learned by one or more persons present)

3. The power gifts
   a. working of miracles (display of supernatural power as the Spirit determines.)
   b. Gifts of healings (different kinds of healings for different kinds of ailments)

The Gift of Faith

    c. Gift of faith (unusual and effective faith poured into the heart and mind by the Spirit)

Somebody probably just got offended because I didn't present the list their way or in the way their religious tradition dictates. Sorry.

The purpose of this chapter is to focus on the gift of faith.

We know that faith itself is a gift because we are saved through faith and the Bible says salvation is a gift. You can never manufacture faith. You can never be good enough to have faith. You can never try hard enough to have faith. You can't recite enough scripture to have faith. You can't pray long enough to get faith. Faith won't come until God pours it into your heart.

"For by grace are ye saved through faith; and that not of yourselves: it is the gift of God: Not of works, lest any man should boast." (Ephesians 2:8-9)

The workings of grace are always activated in your life by faith. Remember the woman who pressed through the crowd to touch Jesus' garment (Matthew 9:20-22).

The scripture says virtue (power) went out of Him. Jesus Himself told her that her faith had saved her (Mark 5:25-34).

This woman was healed by her faith. We know she had faith because she said "…If I may touch but his clothes, I shall be whole." (Mark 5:28). The Bible says, "But those things which proceed out of the mouth come forth from the heart; ..." (Matthew 15:18). Your mouth will always reveal what is in your heart. When I am seeking God for healing, I listen to my mouth. When I hear words that indicate I am faltering, I go back to the Father and ask Him to renew the gift of faith He has put in my heart for the healing.

Maybe you find yourself faltering and you think God got disappointed in you and took back the gift of faith after you fumbled. The Bible says God doesn't change His mind and take back His gifts. He has more desire for you to have faith than you realize. You can't please Him without faith and He desires that you please Him. He has a vested interest in giving you faith. You are His child and He wants to bless you.

"For the gifts and calling of God are without repentance." (Romans 11:29)

"But without faith it is impossible to please him: for he that cometh to God must believe that he is, and that he is a rewarder of them that diligently seek him." (Hebrews 11:6)

Maybe you don't think you have a right to ask God to give you a gift of faith. Paul told us to desire spiritual gifts.

The Gift of Faith

"Follow after charity, and desire spiritual gifts, ..." (1 Corinthians 14:1)

Maybe you have asked God to give you a gift of faith for healing and you aren't sure you got it. What do you do? Ask again. If you aren't sure that He will answer, go back to the scriptures. Look up verses that say He desires to give gifts to you.

"If ye then, being evil, know how to give good gifts unto your children, how much more shall your Father which is in heaven give good things to them that ask him?" (Matthew 7:11)

"Wherefore he saith, When he ascended up on high, he led captivity captive, and gave gifts unto men." (Ephesians 4:8)

When you are convinced that the Bible says God will give you gifts, ask for a gift of faith again. Don't quit asking until you are sure you have heard from the Lord. Remember Jesus' teaching of the persistent woman. She didn't give up until the Judge heard her case and gave her justice.

"..., There was in a city a judge, which feared not God, neither regarded man: And there was a widow in that city; and she came

unto him, saying, Avenge me of mine adversary. And he would not for a while: but afterward he said within himself, Though I fear not God, nor regard man; Yet because this widow troubleth me, I will avenge her, lest by her continual coming she weary me. And the Lord said, Hear what the unjust judge saith. And shall not God avenge his own elect, which cry day and night unto him, though he bear long with them?" (Luke 18:2-7)

How will you know you have received a gift of faith? When you have received it, there will be no doubt.

"Now faith is the substance of things hoped for, the evidence of things not seen." (Hebrews 11:1)

Years ago, I suffered a back injury. When the Lord convinced me that healing was His desire for me, I became certain of my healing. Be sure, my back still hurt. I didn't try to make it stop hurting. That wasn't my responsibility. I was sure of my healing, so I gave thanks continually to God. I wasn't giving thanks to try to get healed. I was giving thanks because I believed I was already healed. You might say, "What evidence did you have of healing?" I would reply, "My faith." That is what Hebrews 11 means when it says "...the evidence of things not seen." I couldn't see the healing in my body, but it was just a real to me as if I could.

The Gift of Faith

When your healing is real to you, you have received a gift of faith.

I wasn't trying to "get healed". I was healed. The following Sunday in church, I had my hands raised worshiping God when I heard three loud popping noises. I turned to see what had made the noise and realized that my back was completely without pain. As of this writing, it has been about fifteen years and I am still free from pain and difficulty. The first time, I struggled for three months in pain seeking God. Since then, I have been injured a number of times. Each time, I have applied these principles of healing and gotten quick relief. Know that I am not just giving you opinions of what I want to be true. I have walked in these truths for years and have proven them by experience.

You may have heard someone say, "Is it by faith or is it real." The truth is, if it is really faith, the evidence is equally as real. You may have only the evidence of faith for a while. How long will it take? It doesn't matter. If the faith is real, you won't waiver, even if it takes years. I don't believe that exercised faith can fail to do anything but bring relief speedily. I also believe when you learn to give God thanks for what is your by faith, no power in heaven, on earth, or under the earth can keep God's promise from manifesting itself in your body.

Learn to listen to your mouth to check up on your heart. Don't play any word games or mind tricks. Don't be tempted to lie and say there is no physical evidence of the ailment if there really is. God doesn't need for you to cover up for Him. If you catch yourself wavering, go back to the word and then to prayer. Continue in prayer until you know that you know that you know the Lord has heard and given you a gift of faith for your healing.

Don't stop here. In the next chapter, I will discuss the much-misunderstood confession of faith. It is a necessary step to becoming whole. As soon as you are sure of the gift of faith, proceed to the confession of faith.

Chapter 7

The Confession of Faith

Never underestimate the power of words. With a single word a child can be torn down or built up all his life. The right or wrong word in testimony from a courtroom witness stand can free or imprison one for life. God already knew about the life giving and taking power of words. He designed it that way.

"Death and life are in the power of the tongue: and they that love it shall eat the fruit thereof." (Proverbs 18:21)

God even called His son, "The Word".

"In the beginning was the Word, and the Word was with God, and the Word was God. The same was in the beginning with God. All things were made by him; and without him

was not any thing made that was made. In him was life; and the life was the light of men." (John 1:1-4)

"And he was clothed with a vesture dipped in blood: and his name is called The Word of God. And the armies which were in heaven followed him upon white horses, clothed in fine linen, white and clean. And out of his mouth goeth a sharp sword, that with it he should smite the nations: and he shall rule them with a rod of iron: and he treadeth the winepress of the fierceness and wrath of Almighty God. And he hath on his vesture and on his thigh a name written, KING OF KINGS, AND LORD OF LORDS." (Revelation 19:13-16)

As modern man has become less literate and more dependent on visual media, he has drifted from understanding the power of words. Yet, that power remains. The word STOP on a sign causes muscle movement and great effort to halt forward motion (in most people).

Is is not strange that words hold power. God knew that. He made it that way. The first chapter of Genesis shows God creating by the power of speech:

"And God said, Let there be light: and there was light." (Genesis 1:3)

The Confession of Faith

"And God said, Let there be a firmament in the midst of the waters, and let it divide the waters from the waters." (Genesis 1:6)

"And God said, Let the waters under the heaven be gathered together unto one place, and let the dry land appear: and it was so." (Genesis 1:9)

It is interesting that in this day, men are beginning to post the ten commandments in public places such as schools and court rooms. Men are becoming weary of the violence that a valueless society produces. God told us to post His word in sight, so we could fill our minds with it and teach it to our children. He promises to bless our so doing.

"Therefore shall ye lay up these my words in your heart and in your soul, …. And ye shall teach them your children, speaking of them when thou sittest in thine house, and when thou walkest by the way, when thou liest down, and when thou risest up. And thou shalt write them upon the door posts of thine house, and upon thy gates: That your days may be multiplied, and the days of your children, in the land which the LORD sware unto your fathers to give them, as the days of heaven upon the earth." (Deuteronomy 11:18-21)

God goes so far as to promise that His words are life and health.

"My son, attend to my words; incline thine ear unto my sayings. Let them not depart from thine eyes; keep them in the midst of thine heart. For they are life unto those that find them, and health to all their flesh." (Proverbs 4:20-22)

God promises that His word will always accomplish what He intended. The concept that God might say something that doesn't happen is not possible.

"So shall my word be that goeth forth out of my mouth: it shall not return unto me void, but it shall accomplish that which I please, and it shall prosper in the thing whereto I sent it." (Isaiah 55:11)

As we become aware of Christ living in us, we should become aware of the power our words invoke. The Bible tells us that God doesn't share his glory with "another" (Isaiah 42:8). The message of the gospel is that we are not "another". God has made us one with Him through His son Jesus (John 15:4). Our words now have creative power.

"For verily I say unto you, That whosoever shall say unto this mountain, Be thou removed, and be thou cast into the sea; and shall not doubt in his heart, but shall believe that those things which he saith shall come to pass; he shall have whatsoever he saith. Therefore I say unto you, What things soever ye desire, when ye pray, believe that ye receive them, and ye shall have them." (Mark 11:23-24)

Please note that the "saying" in this passage follows the "believing". You don't get stuff just because you say it. You must believe it first. As I said in the previous chapter of this book, the believing occurs because of a gift from God. There are conditions on the receiving, such as loving, giving, bearing fruit, asking for what God desires you to have. These must all be met before the "saying" works for you.

In recent years, the so-called "Faith" or "Word" movement used these verses. They were not wrong in their understanding of this scripture. They did frequently fail to note the necessity of faith preceding "speaking". Many who followed after them confused the message into "Say it and get it. Name it and claim it." They mistakenly believed that whatever they wanted would become theirs if they were just consistent in saying that it was theirs. Sometimes faith will rise up in your heart as you confess or say a thing that is in agreement with God's desire for you. But consider that you had to already know God's desire in the matter to know what to say. I would suggest that persons with this experience had already received faith in their hearts as a gift from God. Remember:

"So then faith cometh by hearing, and hearing by the word of God." (Romans 10:17)

First we hear the word, the living Word, in our hearts. Then, faith comes. Then confession follows.

To further emphasize this principle, I will speak of salvation. We know from the scriptures that a person must confess faith with his mouth to be saved. A person on trial cannot give a confession to the court of something he does not know. In the same way, the surety of salvation must be known and then confessed.

"But what saith it? The word is nigh thee, even in thy mouth, and in thy heart: that is, the word of faith, which we preach; That if thou shalt confess with thy mouth the Lord Jesus, and shalt believe in thine heart that God hath raised him from the dead, thou shalt be saved. For with the heart man believeth unto righteousness; and with the mouth confession is made unto salvation." (Romans 10:8-10)

In an effort to properly focus my confession of faith, I begin with the confession as thanksgiving. If I need healing for a particular ailment, I pray, asking the Lord for healing. I continue in prayer, asking for the healing I need until sense in my heart that the Lord has answered and given me faith to believe for the particular healing. This faith comes easily because the Lord said He heals me (Exodus 15:26, Psalms 103:3) and He promised to deliver whatever I ask for if He has already said I can have it (1 John 5:14-15). Knowing this promise and sensing faith rising within my heart, the words of my mouth shift from supplication (asking for healing) to thanksgiving (acknowledging healing). I continue in the confession of thanksgiving until I am certain of His provision. Then my confession will include statements to other believers of what God has done.

"In every thing give thanks: for this is the will of God in Christ Jesus concerning you."
(1 Thessalonians 5:18)

Be sure satan will try to steal what God gives you. He will continually try to find fault with you and will accuse you before God. Notice that the scriptures say we overcome him by the blood of the Lamb and with words.

"Be sober, be vigilant; because your adversary the devil, as a roaring lion, walketh about, seeking whom he may devour:"
(1 Peter 5:8)

"And I heard a loud voice saying in heaven, Now is come salvation, and strength, and the kingdom of our God, and the power of his Christ: for the accuser of our brethren is cast down, which accused them before our God day and night. And they overcame him by the blood of the Lamb, and by the word of their testimony; and they loved not their lives unto the death." (Revelation 12:10-11)

Are the things you say important?

Yes they are.

If you slip and say something negative will you lose your healing?

Your healing was secured by the death of Jesus on the cross. He will not slip. If you do, He will bear you up. You do need to "order you conversation aright" (Psalms 50:23). This means get your life right and well as your speech. It means taking control of your thoughts. It means deciding to think God's way and not listen to your fears. Your fear will say, "But what if you get worse?" God's word says, "And the prayer of faith shall save the sick, and the Lord shall raise him up; and if he have committed sins, they shall be forgiven him. (James 5:15)". This is war. Fight it God's way!

"For though we walk in the flesh, we do not war after the flesh: (For the weapons of our warfare are not carnal, but mighty through

God to the pulling down of strong holds;) Casting down imaginations, and every high thing that exalteth itself against the knowledge of God, and bringing into captivity every thought to the obedience of Christ;" (2 Corinthians 10:3-5)

So if you mess up, do you quit? NO! Go back to the Father. Repent. Tell Him you blew it and ask Him to forgive you. If necessary, ask for healing again. Start at the beginning as often as you must. Hang on to your confession for your life. If your friends laugh at you, find some friends who won't. If you are sunburned, you stay out of the sun. If you are mocked, go somewhere else. I don't care what someone else says about me as long as I am healed! It is not their body. If you die, they may grieve, but they won't die with you. Jesus already died for you. Now let Him live through you!

Chapter 8

The Origin of Sickness

I often hear people talk about sickness as if it somehow serves God's purpose. To begin with, you must see that sickness comes into the world as a result of separation from God. The separation is caused by sin. Therefore, sickness comes from sin.

Jesus was aware of this. He told the man He healed at the pool called Bethesda to avoid future sin to stay well.

"Afterward Jesus findeth him in the temple, and said unto him, Behold, thou art made whole: sin no more, lest a worse thing come unto thee." (John 5:14)

James understood the roll of sin in sickness.

"And the prayer of faith shall save the sick, and the Lord shall raise him up; and if he have

committed sins, they shall be forgiven him. Confess your faults one to another, and pray one for another, that ye may be healed. The effectual fervent prayer of a righteous man availeth much." (James 5:15-16)

Modern translations use the word "sins" where the King James Version says faults. Confess your sins to be healed. This is strong indication that the people who wrote the Bible knew that sin causes sickness.

Perhaps Jesus gave the most proving evidence that sickness is caused by sin when He was in a house at Capernaum. Four men brought a sick man on a mat and tore a hole in the roof of the house to lower him to Jesus.

"And when they could not come nigh unto him for the press, they uncovered the roof where he was: and when they had broken it up, they let down the bed wherein the sick of the palsy lay. When Jesus saw their faith, he said unto the sick of the palsy, Son, thy sins be forgiven thee. But there was certain of the scribes sitting there, and reasoning in their hearts, Why doth this man thus speak blasphemies? who can forgive sins but God only? And immediately when Jesus perceived in his spirit that they so reasoned within themselves, he said unto them, Why reason ye these things in your hearts? Whether is it easier to say to the sick

The Origin of Sickness

of the palsy, Thy sins be forgiven thee; or to say, Arise, and take up thy bed, and walk? But that ye may know that the Son of man hath power on earth to forgive sins, (he saith to the sick of the palsy,) I say unto thee, Arise, and take up thy bed, and go thy way into thine house. And immediately he arose, took up the bed, and went forth before them all;" (Mark 2:4-12)

Today, many modern religionists need to hear Jesus say, "Which is better to say, your sins are forgiven or get up and walk."

Jesus was simply walking in the light of the Word of God given centuries before. Sin always brought sickness. Forgiveness always brought healing.

When the Israelites sinned against God, thousands were struck with the plague and died. Aaron ran between the living and the dead with incense to intercede with God for them (Numbers 16:47). The verdict was death to all because of sin, then life for all protected by an atonement (that which makes amends and brings reconciliation with God). In the next chapter, I will explore the atonement God provided for us in the death of His son Jesus on the cross, but before atonement can be accepted as the cure, sin must be accepted as the cause.

From the very beginning, God told His people that sickness was judgement for their sin. Consider the following passage from Deuteronomy:

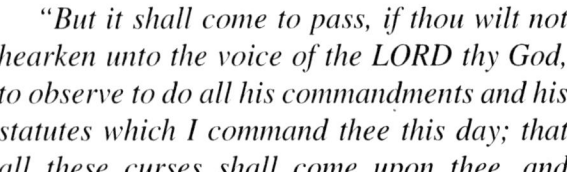

"But it shall come to pass, if thou wilt not hearken unto the voice of the LORD thy God, to observe to do all his commandments and his statutes which I command thee this day; that all these curses shall come upon thee, and overtake thee: ... " (Deuteronomy 28:15)

"Cursed shall be the fruit of thy body, ..." (Deuteronomy 28:18)

"The LORD shall make the pestilence cleave unto thee, until he have consumed thee from off the land, whither thou goest to possess it. The LORD shall smite thee with a consumption, and with a fever, and with an inflammation, and with an extreme burning,... " (Deuteronomy 28:21-22)

"The LORD will smite thee with the botch of Egypt, and with the emerods, and with the scab, and with the itch, whereof thou canst not be healed. The LORD shall smite thee with madness, and blindness, and astonishment of heart:" (Deuteronomy 28:27-28)

With this is mind, consider that all sickness is the result of sin. You might say, "But what about the diseases doctors have identified?" I would answer,

The Origin of Sickness

when the causes of a disease are identified, we have simply identified the agent of sickness introduced into our world by sin that caused the absence of the power of God. Would diseases have existed if God's presence weren't hindered in our lives? I choose to believe not.

The sin causing sickness in your own body may be sin you have committed or sin committed by others. Sin taints mankind to many generations. The effects of that sin, sickness and separation from God, also extend to subsequent generations. This is seen in the following scripture passages:

" ... for I the LORD thy God am a jealous God, visiting the iniquity of the fathers upon the children unto the third and fourth generation of them that hate me;" (Exodus 20:5)

" ... visiting the iniquity of the fathers upon the children, and upon the children's children, unto the third and to the fourth generation." (Exodus 34:7)

"And they that are left of you shall pine away in their iniquity in your enemies' lands; and also in the iniquities of their fathers shall they pine away with them." (Leviticus 26:39)

"The LORD is longsuffering, and of great mercy, forgiving iniquity and transgression, and by no means clearing the guilty, visiting the iniquity of the fathers upon the children unto the third and fourth generation." (Numbers 14: 18)

These and other passages show that God does allow the effect of sin, punishment, to extend to future generations. Mankind is so full of the effects of sin now that we see the massive suffering regularly in our news reports. The sin of the individual obviously is just as capable of bringing punishment.

Some scholars insist that God does not visit guilt for the sin of the fathers on the sons anymore. They quote:

"What mean ye, that ye use this proverb concerning the land of Israel, saying, The fathers have eaten sour grapes, and the children's teeth are set on edge? As I live, saith the Lord GOD, ye shall not have occasion any more to use this proverb in Israel." (Ezekiel 18:2-3)

"The soul that sinneth, it shall die. The son shall not bear the iniquity of the father, neither shall the father bear the iniquity of the son: the righteousness of the righteous shall be

upon him, and the wickedness of the wicked shall be upon him. But if the wicked will turn from all his sins that he hath committed, and keep all my statutes, and do that which is lawful and right, he shall surely live, he shall not die." (Ezekiel 18:20-21)

If you pause and meditate on this scripture for a moment, you will see that it doesn't say God has changed His ways. The sins of the father still visit the son, but only the sons who have not turned from their wicked ways. This is why Jesus said, " Sin no more".

People will spend hours telling you all they have been told by their various doctors. They will give you the classic organ recital, telling you of all their internal woes. They seldom tell you of their sins and repent. If you want healing, start confessing. Make a clean breast of it. Let the Lord get to all the deep-seated sin hidden away in your dusty memories so you can be set free and healed.

Now, I know that someone is thinking, "What about the blind man Jesus said wasn't blind because of his own sin or the sin of his parents?" Jesus said that his condition was so that the work of God might be displayed in his life (John 9:1-3). Jesus did not say that the blindness had no relationship to sin. He simply said that his blindness was not caused by the man's own sin or the sin of his parents. The Jews who questioned Jesus were scripturally correct to look for sin as the cause of blindness. Jesus looked beyond the man and his immediate family and saw the sinful condition of man that brought judgement on man. He thereby saw this as an opportunity for God to exhibit his great love and compassion.

I have experienced God's great love and compassion in my own life as it brought healing to my body. At these times, I was not particularly aware of a particular sin or sinful condition needing treatment. I was aware of my need (pain) and sought the Father's kind touch. He reached out and provided all I needed. Two of these experiences bear repeating here to evidence the truth of what I have been telling you about sin causing sickness and Jesus bring healing and forgiveness.

A number of years ago, I helped a coworker pick up a desk and hurt my back. By lunchtime, I was having trouble walking up stairs. By nighttime, I was in severe pain. This happened on a Friday, so I had the entire weekend to recover! I lay on my back in pain for most of the day Saturday. On Sunday, I got up and went to church. I could hardly stand the twenty-five mile drive home. I knew I needed help immediately because my job required that I spend many hours in my car traveling between customer sites.

On Monday morning I went to work with the confidence that the Lord was my healer. That morning, I received a large shipment of computer equipment to be unpacked and installed. I attacked the pile of boxes saying, "If you are going to be healed, you must act healed!" I was fine as I unpacked the equipment and installed it. Only later in the day did I have a problem. A coworker asked me if I went to the hos-

The Origin of Sickness

pital with my back. He knew someone who was injured at work and disabled. Another coworker had a relative who hurt his back at work and was never able to work again. I began to worry. My back started to hurt.

This was the beginning of three months of the most severe pain I have ever known. When your back is badly hurt, there is no comfortable position. Every little move takes a mammoth effort to overcome the pain. Even sitting can bring tears to your eyes. A sneeze can bring agony.

I re-read every scripture I had ever known about healing. I dug out my copies of "Christ the Healer" and other classic books about God's heal power. I tried anything I could think of. I prayed without ceasing. I confessed everything I could think of. I even tried to exercise my back in "faith" that it would be restored. Nothing I could do seemed to help. During this time I did become convinced that I could be healed if only I knew what to do.

One day during my ordeal, God spoke to me; yes me, just a nobody. He said, "Your healing is provided in the atonement. I would no more leave you sick that I would leave you in sin." It struck me that the act Jesus performed on the cross was enough for sin and the consequences of sin then, now, and forever. As of that moment, I didn't care if my body ever quit hurting. The healing of Jesus became a reality in my spirit. I told the Lord, "Lord, I don't care if my back is healed in a day, or ten days, or a year, or ten thousand years, as far as I am concerned, it is already done because I believe it in my spirit."

The following Sunday in church, I had my arms raised praising God. I am used to ignoring the fatigue of my arms when I worship, so I ignored the pain in my back and praised God with all I had. I was so overjoyed just to know him. I wasn't saying , "Lord heal me", or "Lord thank you for healing me." I was simply saying, "Lord I love you. I worship you. I adore you. I thank you for your son Jesus, for his death on the cross so that I can know you." Then it happened! My back popped three times. The pops were so loud that I looked around to see what happened. When I heard the pops, I felt my spine move just like three large hands pushed it into perfect alignment. When I looked around, I immediately notice that the pain was completely gone.

You might ask, did it last. I will tell you now that any healing you receive from the Lord will be tested. It will not be tested by God, but by the enemy of God who doesn't want you to be loved. It wasn't long before my back began to hurt again. As I began to pray, the Holy Spirit impressed me to place my hand on my back and rebuke the pain. I commanded the pain and all of it's causes to leave. It left. As of this writing, I have commanded pain to leave my back at least a dozen times. Each time it has left immediately. For the past fifteen years, my back has been strong and healthy, thanks to the atonement of Jesus on the cross.

The second biggest healing I have ever received had to do with job related stress. I was suffering from chronic indigestion, colon spasms, and hemorrhoids. Not only was this unpleasant, it was downright

The Origin of Sickness

painful. I received good advise about surgery, so I went calling on the master surgeon. I would like to tell you that I found healing immediately. I didn't.

I did get relief enough to go on a camping trip with my family. After we returned from the trip, the trouble and pain returned. I did all I could by fleshly means. I quit abusing my digestive tract with coffee and caffeine. I got some relief, but still suffered. As I continued to pray, my spiritual eyes began to turn upward, toward the Lord. I remembered what He taught me years earlier when He healed my back. I prayed to the Lord for healing until I heard Him speaking to my spirit saying, "You have been healed." I then began to worship Him for the healing He had given. Within the next several days, my condition continued to improve. I didn't pay much attention to my condition, but just kept praising the Lord for what my spirit already knew was done. I was driving to work one morning, singing in the Spirit, when the Lord touched me and completed the healing.

Like every other healing I have received, this one has been tested. I simply command the condition and it's causes to leave and begin to thank the Lord for His atonement and my deliverance from sin and the consequences of sin. The problem goes away quickly. Once the healing is done, there is no reason to suffer a long time trying to hold on to it. Healing is yours. It is done. Thank God vigorously; rejoicing in the victory you have already won.

Chapter 9

The Atonement

To atone simply means to make amends or to satisfy someone's claim or to make reparation for an offense or injury. The literal old English meaning was to make "at - one". In other words, remove separation and join together.

The religious meaning of atonement is "to make one with God."

You can think of atonement in at least two ways. As satisfying a deficit, or as a peace offering.

If my life was a checkbook and I came up short when I balanced my account, someone could give me the cash necessary to bring my account into balance. They would have satisfied the deficit in my account. They would have restored my balance. God knew my life would be "out of balance", so He satisfies my deficit with the blood of His own son, Jesus.

The thing that has my life upset is sin. It separates me from the continual blessing of God needed to live a full, contented life. Many people think they have satisfied themselves with their education or wealth, but their security is often crumbled by the difficulties of life. The only way I can repair the breach between God and me is through the offering of the blood of His son Jesus.

One of the earliest illustrations of the atonement of Jesus on the cross is an experience the Israelites had in the wilderness.

> *"And they journeyed from mount Hor by the way of the Red sea, to compass the land of Edom: and the soul of the people was much discouraged because of the way. And the people spake against God, and against Moses, Wherefore have ye brought us up out of Egypt to die in the wilderness? for there is no bread, neither is there any water; and our soul loatheth this light bread. And the LORD sent fiery serpents among the people, and they bit the people; and much people of Israel died. Therefore the people came to Moses, and said, We have sinned, for we have spoken against the LORD, and against thee; pray unto the LORD, that he take away the serpents from us. And Moses prayed for the people. And the LORD said unto Moses, Make thee a fiery serpent, and set it upon a pole: and it shall come to pass, that every one that is bitten, when he looketh upon it, shall live. And Moses made a serpent of brass, and put it upon a pole, and it came to pass, that if a serpent had bitten any man, when he beheld the serpent of brass, he lived." (Numbers 21:4-9)*

The Atonement

This experience of the snake lifted up on the pole is mentioned again in the New Testament. Jesus shows us that He is God's provision for our deliverance.

※

"And as Moses lifted up the serpent in the wilderness, even so must the Son of man be lifted up: That whosoever believeth in him should not perish, but have eternal life." (John 3:14-15)

Jesus became our deliverance by taking a curse upon Him. By taking the punishment for something He didn't do, He relieved us from requiring any punishment for our crimes against God.

※

"Christ hath redeemed us from the curse of the law, being made a curse for us: for it is written, Cursed is every one that hangeth on a tree:" (Galatians 3:13)

Established law required shed blood to cover sin. Jesus' shed blood is what redeems us. It is what gets forgiveness for our sins. His blood defeats our foe, satan.

※

"And almost all things are by the law purged with blood; and without shedding of blood is no remission." (Hebrews 9:22)

"In whom we have redemption through his blood, even the forgiveness of sins:" (Colossians 1:14)

"...Jesus Christ, ...washed us from our sins in his own blood,..." (Revelation 1:5)

"And I said unto him, Sir, thou knowest. And he said to me, These are they which came out of great tribulation, and have washed their robes, and made them white in the blood of the Lamb." (Revelation 7:14)

"And the great dragon was cast out, that old serpent, called the Devil, and Satan, which deceiveth the whole world: he was cast out into the earth, and his angels were cast out with him. And I heard a loud voice saying in heaven, Now is come salvation, and strength, and the kingdom of our God, and the power of his Christ: for the accuser of our brethren is cast down, which accused them before our God day and night. And they overcame him by the blood of the Lamb, and by the word of their testimony; and they loved not their lives unto the death." (Revelation 12:9-11)

The Atonement

Isn't it interesting that the blood sacrifice is central to so many religions? Even religions that don't recognize Jesus have an understanding of atonement. Some religions try to profane the use of blood by drinking blood. This is strictly forbidden in Old Testament law. The writers of the law did not know that blood carried disease. They only knew the instruction of God.

The fact that His cruel death on the cross provides healing as well as salvation was foretold by Isaiah and called back to account by Peter. When Jesus was flogged, strips of flesh were torn loose from His back. His back became striped by the punishment He bore for us.

"But he was wounded for our transgressions, he was bruised for our iniquities: the chastisement of our peace was upon him; and with his stripes we are healed." (Isaiah 53:5)

"Who his own self bare our sins in his own body on the tree, that we, being dead to sins, should live unto righteousness: by whose stripes ye were healed." (1 Peter 2:24)

I am going to tell you a tale of what God has been up to without giving all the scripture references at this time. Just bear with me. If you disagree with me, it won't hurt my feelings. I am just offering this tale in an effort to explain the purpose of atonement.

God created heavenly creatures for His amusement and glory. There are various winged creatures that constantly proclaim His majesty. He also created servants, called angels. These servants have the appearance of large men. Some are quite beautiful.

Some of the angels were created to lead groups of other angels. One such leader became proud of his beauty and strength and decided to exalt himself above God. He started a revolt in God's kingdom. God drove this angelic leader, satan, out of His heaven. Satan took with him a large number of angels who had joined his rebellion against God. These were cast down to the earth. Today they roam the earth, seeking people to demonize.

God decided to show satan His magnificence. He created man in his image. Man was created so that through his relationship with God, satan could see God's limitless wisdom and love. Satan deceived man into rebellion, so God had to banish man to the earth. God continued to speak to man and instruct him in spiritual things.

After man had gained some understanding, God established a ritual of blood sacrifice. A spotless lamb was killed and offered for man's sin. Satan scoffed at the sacrifice. Basically, he said, "Go ahead with your sacrifice. I can still steal man away from you!"

The animal sacrifice continued for years as God toiled with man until man learned to hold on to God. Man finally learned to not worship stone and metal. He learned that there is one God.

When man's religion was ready, God sent His

The Atonement

own son. Because the Holy Spirit conceived Him in the womb of a virgin, He owed his bloodline to God and not man. Because He was born human, He was flesh and blood. He was a new creation, God and man. He lived a sinless life among men, showing them the very image of God.

When the time was right, God allowed satan to kill His Son. Because He had never sinned, His death was undeserved. As a result, He was able to come back to life. He now has a payment for the debt of sin greater than any sin because His is the blood of a perfect sacrifice. He is the spotless Lamb

Because satan accepted God's terms as He unfolded them, satan is bound by spiritual law to release anyone whose sin is paid for by this perfect offering. God tricked satan. He didn't lie. Satan assumed he knew what God was up to and thought he was more clever than God. He was wrong.

We are made free from sin and the consequences of sin (including disease) because Jesus died on the cross. When He said, "It is finished." that is what He meant. There is no other sacrifice needed to pay the price. I don't have to suffer to pay the price. I don't have to die to pay the price. The atonement is complete in Jesus.

When I was a young Christian, the Holy Spirit gave a picture representing the atonement. I was praying intently about some need and had the impression that my prayers were bouncing off the ceiling. Then, the Spirit gave me a picture of a downpour of blood that would have drenched me like a heavy rain. Immediately, I was aware that the Lord was listening intently to my prayer! Just as in the ancient temple, blood was shed between man and the holy place, today we must come through the blood to enter into God's presence. The Bible says Jesus entered the Holy Place in heaven with His own blood as an offering. He only had to offer His blood once. The blood of bulls and goats had to be offered over and over again and even so couldn't take away sin (Hebrews 10:1-4).

"But Christ being come an high priest of good things to come, by a greater and more perfect tabernacle, not made with hands, that is to say, not of this building; Neither by the blood of goats and calves, but by his own blood he entered in once into the holy place, having obtained eternal redemption for us." (Hebrews 9:11-12)

"But this man, after he had offered one sacrifice for sins for ever, sat down on the right hand of God;" (Hebrews 10:12)

The Old Testament story of Abraham's obedience to God's command to offer Isaac, the son of promise, teaches us an aspect of atonement. Abraham fully intended to offer his son. The Lord sent him, but then stopped him before he could complete the act. The Lord also sent a ram, caught in the thicket, as a substitute offering (Genesis 22:1-18). The name Abraham called God in that place, Jehovah-jireh, means God provides. This is an aspect of atonement we must see. Not only must there be atonement, but God must provide the atonement. We can never do anything significant enough to make atonement with God. Only the atonement provided by God is sufficient.

Jesus is sufficient sacrifice to clean us of all sin. His sacrifice was complete and effective. It only had to be made once. Having made the sacrifice, He remains in the presence of God as a constant reminder of the atonement He has made for us. We have full confidence to enter God's presence through the blood of Jesus (Hebrews 10:19).

Chapter 10

Learning How to Receive

So, if the atonement provides for my healing and if it is truly finished, why am I still sick? I recently put some money on an on-line account for payment to someone else. For days, he didn't claim the payment. It was his to have, but he couldn't use that money until he claimed it. God has made a deposit in your heavenly account. You have the power of withdrawal for all your needs, including healing. The action of withdrawing that deposit is your responsibility. God won't leave you ignorant of the deposit. That is why I am writing these words. He will tell you, "Here it is, come and get it!"

The Bible says you will eat the good of the land if you are "willing and obedient (some translations say "willing and able")." (Isaiah 1:19). It is not enough to be surrounded by good stuff. You must pick it up and eat.

The requirement of action on our part to receive what God has provided is nowhere more evident than in the receiving of salvation. I know some people say God does all the work of salvation, but I disagree. I believe God defends your ability to choose or refuse. The Bible says what we must do to be saved. The first thing is to believe. The second is to confess. This should be a familiar pattern by now. The whole principle of receiving healing that I have been expounding via the death of so many trees is based on this principle.

"For with the heart man believeth unto righteousness; and with the mouth confession is made unto salvation." (Romans 10:10)

Many have been influenced by traditional religious false humility. They say, "I am just a sinner saved by grace, I am not worthy to receive." This makes God out to be a liar. It is true that you have sinned. "All have sinned" (Romans 3:23). "If we say we have no sin, we lie" (1 John 1:8). It is just as true that if we confess our sin, God removes even the foul stench of sin from us!

"If we confess our sins, he is faithful and just to forgive us our sins, and to cleanse us from all unrighteousness. If we say that we have not sinned, we make him a liar, and his word is not in us. My little children, these things write I unto you, that ye sin not. And if any man sin, we have an advocate with the Father, Jesus Christ the righteous:" (1 John 1:9-2:1)

"Confess your faults one to another, and pray one for another, that ye may be healed. The effectual fervent prayer of a righteous man availeth much." (James 5:16)

God doesn't leave you dirtied up by sin. He cleans you up by the power of His Son's shed blood. Before He was crucified, Jesus prayed to the Father that the Father would sanctify His disciples (John 17:017). To sanctify means to "set apart for sacred purpose or holy use". Jesus wants us holy in the eyes of God!

Many have been taught that to claim holiness is to steal God's glory. They quote:

" ...I will not give my glory unto another." (Isaiah 48:11)

Jesus acknowledged the Glory of God. He then laid claim to that glory as His own. He went on to say that He was glorified in us! Here we are, afraid that we are stealing God's glory when all the while, we ARE God's glory!

"I have glorified thee on the earth: I have finished the work which thou gavest me to do. And now, O Father, glorify thou me with thine own self with the glory which I had with thee before the world was." (John 17:4-5)

"I pray for them: I pray not for the world, but for them which thou hast given me; for they are thine. And all mine are thine, and thine are mine; and I am glorified in them." (John 17:910)

How does a ray of sunlight glorify the sun from whence it came? It points back to the sun. Our glory comes from the Son of God. Therefore, we must continually point back to the Son. The lesson Jesus taught us here is that we are not "another". We are one with Him, bearing His name, sharing His glory.

When I continually tell people that God healed me, I am not suggesting that I am so super that I got healed. I am telling them that God is so super that I got healed. I am no more righteous than any other believer. We are all made righteous by application of the cleansing blood of Jesus.

Decide right now that if Jesus said you are His glory, you are worth healing.

Don't fall prey to false humility. The devil wants you to go around saying things like, "I am just suffering for Jesus. I am just a Job for God."

Don't be suckered into this sin of pride. Exalting yourself to any extreme is wrong. If you exalt your self as an extreme example of suffering, you do so because it makes you proud.

Isn't it enough for you that you are Jesus' glory? Decide now to quit proclaiming your own low estate and begin proclaiming the glory of God, revealed in Jesus, and extended to those who believe. To be proud is to stand in the spotlight. Get out of the spotlight or you will lose God's blessing.

"But he giveth more grace. Wherefore he saith, God resisteth the proud, but giveth grace unto the humble." (James 4:6)

If you go to someone's house and see birthday presents on their table, you don't open them just because it is your birthday. If you see your name on the presents, that changes things. You now expect to open them. Look in the scripture and see the glory God has poured all over you through Jesus and realize that not only is it your birthday, your name has been changed to a new name indicating that you are one with Jesus. Your new name is all over the presents. God wants you to rip the paper off and have His best!

If you pass the obstacle of believing that you deserve healing because of what Jesus is in you, then you only lack the next step where you seize hold of what He offers.

Chapter 11

How the Kingdom Works

It isn't enough to know that God wants you healed. It isn't enough to get right with God, removing all obstacles to healing. There is always a point where you must seize hold of the healing.

You have to be like a man who falls overboard from an ocean liner. Even if someone throws him a lifeline, the ship can't stop immediately. He must hang on for dear life while the ship comes to a stop. You must be just as determined to hang on to the healing of God until you are pulled safely aboard His vessel.

In the words of Jesus:

"And from the days of John the Baptist until now the kingdom of heaven suffereth violence, and the violent take it by force." (Matthew 11:12)

Other translations use the word "force" instead of

violence. Either way, people who seize hold of it obtain the kingdom of God.

In the words of Paul:

"Fight the good fight of faith, lay hold on eternal life, whereunto thou art also called, and hast professed a good profession before many witnesses." (1 Timothy 6:12)

Ok, I know what you are thinking. Didn't Jesus say the meek would inherit the earth (Matthew 5:5)?

I fully believe in being meek when dealing with other people. Love requires that I keep no record of the wrongs done to me. It also requires that I seek to bless my enemies and not curse them.

This is not a forcefulness when dealing with other people. This is a forcefulness when wrestling with the spiritual enemies that try to steal away the seed of blessing God just scattered on our bodies.

"For we wrestle not against flesh and blood, but against principalities, against powers, against the rulers of the darkness of this world, against spiritual wickedness in high places. Wherefore take unto you the whole armour of God, that ye may be able to withstand in the evil day, and having done all, to stand." (Ephesians 6:12-13)

If satan won't leave you alone to share God's

message of salvation without trying to oppose you, he also won't leave you alone to be healed without opposing you.

I have never had a healing that satan didn't try to steal away. First come the whispered questions and doubts. Then come the outright lies about God. I am inclined to back him into a corner and shout in his face, "No you don't. I won't hear any lies about my Jesus, the power of His blood, or how much He loves me and provides for me!"

If I can jump to my feet at a ball game and yell "Yes!" when my team scores, then I can jump to my spiritual feet and yell "Thank you for healing me!" when I realize that God is pouring out His healing.

Are you afraid of what other people might think? If they have a problem, just let them sit there in their disease. You get to your feet and shout thanks to God and be healed.

But people didn't yell at Jesus when He healed them, did they?

When Jesus healed ten lepers, only one came back to worship Him. The Bible says he glorified God with a loud voice. The Bible also says He was made whole. I am not sure what that means. Did he get his fingers and lips back when the others didn't? I really don't know. I do know that Jesus was particularly moved by the worship. He must have been, He gave it special recognition.

"And one of them, when he saw that he was healed, turned back, and with a loud voice

glorified God, And fell down on his face at his feet, giving him thanks: and he was a Samaritan. And Jesus answering said, Were there not ten cleansed? but where are the nine? There are not found that returned to give glory to God, save this stranger. And he said unto him, Arise, go thy way: thy faith hath made thee whole. " (Luke 17:15-19)

A story is told of Smith Wigglesworth waiting at a bus stop. The story says that a woman was followed to the bus stop by her little dog. At first she sweetly said, "Go home". The dog didn't budge. Finally, when the bus arrived, she stamped her foot and shouted, "Go home!" The dog took off like a shot! The story says that Smith Wigglesworth made a comment that this is the way you must talk to the devil.

Unfortunately, I can't verify this story. It doesn't really matter. I have the story of Jesus and the ten lepers. I have the story of blind Bartimaeus tossing aside his cloak to go to Jesus for healing (Mark 10:50). I have the story of the woman with the issue of blood pressing in through the crowd because she believed that if she could only touch the edge of His garment, she would be healed (Matthew 9:20). There are many true stories of the help people got when they reached out forcefully toward Jesus.

Chapter 12

Let's Hear That Again

Now that I have shared with you the approach and methods that I have used successfully to obtain healing for many years, I want to review these teachings to help bring them into focus. Bear with me if I become somewhat analytical in my method at this point. I am just trying to provide some structure that will help you get on track and stay on track as you seek God for healing in your own body.

If you have questions about the steps outlined here, go back to the particular chapter of the book that addresses the step and read it again. These are not long chapters (on purpose!). It shouldn't take long to review and master the technique.

The major key is that if God doesn't heal you, you won't get healed. Don't become lost in the method. Become aware of the Father. Don't become enamored with the technique; become overwhelmed by Jesus and His great gift. Don't become a dry analytical, become an exultant receiver!

Step 1—Change Yourself

Ask God to show you where you need to change. I have never met anyone who couldn't improve with God's help. This very moment, after experiencing God's healing power this very week, I can still see changes I need to make in my life so I can be closer to Him. Make the effort. Get the reward!

Step 2—Be Sure God Wants You Healed

If you have any lingering doubts, get a concordance and look up all the scriptures about healing. If nothing else, read Matthew, Mark, Luke, and John. Read what the Bible has to say about all the miracles Jesus worked. If you are confused about Paul's thorn in the flesh, look the passage up (2 Corinthians 12). The Bible tells what it was. It wasn't sickness. The man was beaten, starved, shipwrecked, etc. If you are trying to identify with Job, remind yourself that Jesus has purged your sin (Hebrews 1:3).

Step 3—Trust The Bible

Let the Bible be the authority. Don't trust the opinions of men who take traditions outside the Bible and use them to tell you what God desires. Regardless of what approach you take to the integrity of the Bible, you must believe the message

God has left there for you if you want to touch God. Otherwise, you won't know where to find Him.

Step 4—Learn How Faith Works and Apply It

Ask God for healing. Don't try to go on to the other steps until you know you have faith in your heart. When you know it is yours, begin to give thanks continually. As of this writing, I was suffering an ailment. Before I got to this chapter, I began to give God thanks for what I already knew in my heart He had done. The pain and suffering left. When you follow the Bible plan (see Mark 11:24-25), nothing in heaven, on the earth, or under the earth can keep you from receiving what you know in your heart God has given and confess as true with your mouth.

Step 5—Hear God's Voice

God speaks all the time. We just don't listen. If you have reached the point where hearing God is more important to you than any other thing, you will take time to get quiet and get right with Him.

Go to prayer and seek God's blessing until you hear Him saying that what you are requesting is yours. If you aren't sure He spoke to you, continue to seek until you hear. If you continue to be unsure, got back to the earlier steps, especially reading the

Bible and finding out what God has to say about healing.

Step 6—Learn How to Know When God Has Given You Faith

Knowing that all faith comes as a gift from God, learn how to recognize faith in your own heart. It may be confidence. It may be peace. It may be joy. Whatever form it takes, learn to recognize when the gift has come in your heart.

Also, learn how to tell if you have let your faith weaken. If you begin to doubt, you will sink in the water just like Peter did when he took his eyes off Jesus and looked at the wind and the waves (Matthew 14:30).

Monitor the words of your mouth. They will reveal the contents of your heart. Don't just change your words to try to make faith happen. Go back to the earlier steps. Read the Bible verses. Seek God again. When you know that faith has come, give thanks continually. If your words reveal weakness again, start over. Do it again and again until you get it right! Your mouth will always tell you what is in your heart (Matthew 12:34). If your heart isn't correctly aligned, you might as well start over. Remember, healing starts in the heart (or spirit) and then manifests in the flesh, just like your salvation.

Step 7 –Confess Your Faith

Start with thanksgiving. Tell the Father "Thank you." for your healing. Tell Jesus "Thank you." for dying on the cross in your place. When you have been able to go day after day without wavering, begin to tell your friends what God has done.

Start with the people that you know respect God and love you. Don't bother with people who are prone to doubt at first. Start with the safe ones. After a while, when you can handle it, confess your healing to the hard cases. Listen for the encouragement of the Holy Spirit and let Him help you sort out who to tell and who to avoid. Don't tell everyone immediately or they will discourage you and try to get you to give up.

It always puzzles me when people who love you try to get you to give up on God and just be sick. They have accepted the weird idea that you must be sick so you should just accept it. If they really believed this way, they wouldn't go to the doctor. They are just confused. Don't let them confuse you.

Step 8—Understand the Source of Sickness

If you still aren't sure that sickness comes from sin, you need to read the Bible. You may have to decide that you want healing strongly enough to abandon human religious traditions that have kept you sick. This step is critical. If your doctor doesn't know what is making you sick, he can't do anything for you but guess. You need to be sure about this one before you go to the Master Physician.

Step 9—Understand the Cure

Study the concept of punishment required for sin. Study the concept of atonement. See what God has been up to all these thousands of years. It didn't just happen. It isn't some new thing. It is the same old thing, seen with new eyes that have the scales removed. Jesus died for our sins.

Most people don't have a clue about the true meaning of the atonement. In all the years I have been a Christian, I have only heard two sermons about the atonement. If I owed a million dollars and someone handed me a document that would remove my debt, I would read it. The Bible is a document that proves that you are free from sin and the consequences of sin, including sickness and death, because of a price paid by the only one who ever was or ever will be worthy and able to pay, Jesus. If this issue isn't resolved for you now, go read the "deed" God has given you to this new life again and again until it "takes".

Step 10—Prepare Yourself To Receive

Get it through your thick skull that if anyone can have it, you can have it. God wants you healed so badly that He put His Son's name and glory all over you. Quit looking down. Look up and lift the hands that hang down to receive blessing from above.

Step 11—Grab It!

Don't just sit passively by saying, "Well, God can heal me if He wants to." Do you sit around saying, "Well, my children can just go to hell if they want to" or do you get on your knees and fight for them. It is time to fight for your healing. Tell God you aren't going to let go until He blesses you. It won't make Him mad. It will make Him glad. The whole purpose of creation was to make a special people to fellowship with Him. He delights in people who hang on while proclaiming, "I won't let you go, Lord!"

Step 12—Be Blessed

I hope all this effort has kindled a fire in you. I hope you get serious about God. I hope you begin to believe the Bible and get on your knees, NO!, on your face in prayer. I hope you see Jesus, high and lifted up. I hope you feel His sweet presence as the Holy Spirit, the Spirit of Jesus, comes to you and you feel Him wrap you up in His healing. I hope you find the blessing you are seeking, here in this life and then forever in the presence of Jesus and the Father.

In Conclusion:

"...I am the LORD that healeth thee."
(Exodus 15:26)

"O God, thou art my God; early will I seek thee: my soul thirsteth for thee, my flesh longeth for thee in a dry and thirsty land, where no water is; To see thy power and thy glory, so as I have seen thee in the sanctuary. Because thy lovingkindness is better than life, my lips shall praise thee. Thus will I bless thee while I live: I will lift up my hands in thy name. My soul shall be satisfied as with marrow and fatness; and my mouth shall praise thee with joyful lips:" (Psalms 63:1-5)

Statement of Limitations

I am not a licensed medical professional.

I cannot legally give you any instruction or suggestion to discontinue any treatment of a licensed medical professional.

If you are under the care of a licensed medical professional and believe your condition has changed because of an experience in faith, please discuss this experience with the licensed medical professional before making any changes to his or her prescribed treatment.

God is just as able to keep unneeded medications from harming you as He is of healing you. This may be a process you have to work through.

If you are not happy with the results of your consultation with your licensed medical professional, exercise your right to a second opinion. Search for a Christian licensed medical professional who is interested in helping you work through your healing.

If you are not under the care of a licensed medical professional, I cannot advise you to deny yourself such help. God is equally up to the task of helping you work through your healing this way. Again, I suggest you seek a Christian licensed medical professional.

Consult competent sources about diet and exercise. I am not an expert. I would only recommend avoiding strange, fad "remedies" that are commonly available. God is just as able to heal people who eat and exercise wrong as people who eat and exercise right.

Do take care of you body. It has to last until you leave this life.

Healing Log

	Prayed for This Made This Change Heard This From the Lord Got This in My Spirit
Date	Got This Physical Answer

Date	
_____	_____
_____	_____
_____	_____
_____	_____
_____	_____
_____	_____
_____	_____
_____	_____
_____	_____

Date	Prayed for This Made This Change Heard This From the Lord Got This in My Spirit Got This Physical Answer

Date	Prayed for This Made This Change Heard This From the Lord Got This in My Spirit Got This Physical Answer
———	———————————————————
———	———————————————————
———	———————————————————
———	———————————————————
———	———————————————————
———	———————————————————
———	———————————————————
———	———————————————————
———	———————————————————
———	———————————————————
———	———————————————————
———	———————————————————

Date	Prayed for This / Made This Change / Heard This From the Lord / Got This in My Spirit / Got This Physical Answer

Date	Prayed for This Made This Change Heard This From the Lord Got This in My Spirit Got This Physical Answer

Author Contact

**Lawrence Thompson
P.O. Box 711
Boiling Springs, NC 28017**

~~unboundmission@yahoo.com~~

lawrence.thompson@unboundmission.org

Printed in the United States
6053